Bona Vada

Selected Publications by Jeremy Reed

Poetry
Isthmus of Samuel Greenberg (1976)
Bleecker Street (1980)
By The Fisheries (1984)
Nero (1985)
Selected Poems (1987)
Engaging Form (1988)
Nineties (1990)
Red Haired Android (1992)
Kicks (1994)
Pop Stars, with Mick Rock (1995)
Sweet Sister Lyric (1996)
Saint Billie (2000)
Patron Saint of Eyeliner (2000)
Heartbreak Hotel (2002)
Duck and Sally Inside (2006)
Orange Sunshine (2006)
This Is How You Disappear (2007)
West End Survival Kit (2009)
Bona Drag (2009)
Black Russian: Out-takes from the Airmen's Club 1978-9 (2010)
Piccadilly Bongo (with Marc Almond) (2010)

Novels
The Lipstick Boys (1984)
Blue Rock (1987)
Red Eclipse (1989)
Inhabiting Shadows (1990)
Isidore (1991)
When The Whip Comes Down (1992)
Chasing Black Rainbows (1994)
The Pleasure Chateau (1994)
Diamond Nebula (1995)
Red Hot Lipstick (1996)
Sister Midnight (1997)
Dorian (1998)
Boy Caesar (2004)
The Grid (2008)

BONA VADA

Jeremy Reed

Shearsman Books

Published in the United Kingdom in 2011 by
Shearsman Books Ltd
58 Velwell Road
Exeter EX4 4LD

www.shearsman.com

ISBN 978-1-84861-164-1
First Edition

Copyright © Jeremy Reed, 2011.

The right of Jeremy Reed to be identified as the author of this work
has been asserted by him in accordance with the
Copyrights, Designs and Patents Act of 1988.
All rights reserved.

Cover illustration copyright © Luka Young, 2011.
Author photo copyright © Gregory Hesse, 2009.

Contents

Baby's Got a Gun

Book Thieves   11
Tipping Points   12
What's On   13
Blacks and Grays   14
Dusty Springfield's (blues) at 5am   15
My Lives   16
It Takes Two Baby   17
Going Down Slow   18
We All Adore Johnny   20
Thinking of JC (Good Times, Bad Times)   22
Baby's Got a Gun   23
Aliens   24
Prospecting Poet   25

Current Affairs

Alan's Time   29
Opium for Men   31
Back to Bill Franks   32
To a Friend in Despair   33
What the Dead Do   37
Dylanologist   39
e-mailing Edmund White   40
Book Catalogue   41
Somewhere a Change   42
Current Affairs   43
Rewriting Shakespeare's Sonnets   44
You Wear It So Well   45

China Yum Yum

Jaffa Cakes   49
Kitchen Poem   50
The Difference between Harrods' and Fortnum's Smoky Teas   51
China Yum Yum   53
First Out   54
Thundery Blues   56

Sooner or Later Frank	57
Listening to Johnnie Ray in Bed, Baby	58
Dorian Gray: the Physicals	60
Grey Eyes	61

Pop

Pop	65
Lolita	66
Japanese French	68
Moving On	70
Missing You	71
Saint Jamie	72
London/Tokyo	74
Hot and Cold	75
Billy Fury	76
Something the Matter	78
Sisters	79
London My Time	80
Summer in the City	82

Moon Gangs

E. Coli	85
Almost Dark	86
Moon Gangs	87
Antivenom	90

People Who Don't Die

Forgotten Poems	93
Cape Goliard	94
Beautiful Losers	96
Death Tourism	97
Syd's Dead	99
The Last Experience	100
Saint Derek of Dungeness	101
Dungeness Blues	106
White Associations	107
Geography	108
Moondust	109
Baudelaire and the 21st Century	111

'Even in death it's language first.'

Asa Benveniste

Cooked me a spoonful of diamonds
cooked me a spoonful of gold
just one spoon of your precious love
will satisfy my soul

Willie Dixon

For John Robinson and Mark Jackson

BABY'S GOT A GUN

Book Thieves

I never guessed at first, this man
so quizzically attentive to Burroughs—
he'd been in twice, casual knitwear,
sober jeans, academic air,
Boeing aluminium-
coloured hair;
I never thought his slow reconnaissance
of signed Burroughs, Ginsberg and Kerouac,
more than a collector's internal debate
over the price, dust-wrapper, state,
his knowledge worn the way a silver ring
gets eaten by the skin. The third time he
left space where a Burroughs *Naked Lunch* first
in its olive green Olympia imprint
had faced outwards, as though he'd cut a tree
from a familiar stand.
The fourth time, he lacked nerve, or I was quick,
his adrenalin never fired the shot;
the fifth time a signed Kerouac
went missing like a pane of glass
lifted clean from a window frame.
We preferred to live with the enigma
and never questioned him, but I was curious
about his method, as I might
be of a disappearing act,
or something incisive like a surgeon's cut,
or how a chess player conceives
a configurative strategy,
and waited for him to return and show
me how the signed John Fante *Ask The Dust*
left with him, like he'd put on extra weight
he never showed, slipping out casually.

Tipping Points

Magnolias collapse like a pink trifle,
a mashed dessert, get flattened underfoot
in cold abrasive thunder showers. I feel
the planet air-pocket in spin
like a plane thrown about by wind
somewhere above the China sea,
the passengers starting to crawl with sweat.
It's a race between tipping points,
a switch to sustainable technology
or collapse: a network blackout,
all power crashed.
One school holiday, lost in blue mirage
hazing the beach, right down on the green tide
a friend grabbed a rubbery octopus
out of its niche in a rock corridor,
tentacles grabbing, and its black ink cap
projected over his white shirt,
the stain opening out like a continent,
a sort of blackest Africa.
It's the shock I remember, the black squirt
gunned like a missile launcher, and my friend's
momentary shattering against a rock.
It's my three-button black Jaeger blazer
brings it all back, so too the planet's flip
one side light and the other dark,
but angry light-polluted and burnt-out,
things getting rocky, as I track
across a pink magnolia petal littered park.

What's On

Disturbance in the city's hypothalamus—
a new J G Ballard novel, a riff
from a Rolling Stones rehearsal,
a variant chord from the human riff's
indestructible neurology;
and somewhere in a lab, donor oocytes
compounded into human clones,
we'll never know the difference one day,
except the eyes turned blank as cellulose
on a Jaguar XK coupe—
two of them standing by the underground car park
entrance, warrened beneath Bloomsbury Square?
And then the underground UFO factory,
donor organ traffickers, dealers cocktailing psychoactive
additives, new drugs for a new body
redesigned for the visionary present,
the abdication of reality?
A Delta 11 rocket blasts off from Cape Canaveral,
delivering NASA Mars probes, its green casing
logoed with blue and red NASA roundels
bound for the red planet.
The universe weighs in at 10 kilograms per cubic metre,
and me I'm 50 kilograms, that light
in volume, I'm just nerve and personality,
no body mass, stripped-down for easy death
and poetry? The gateway's there
if we could see it—50 years from now,
100, 200, no different from imagining
its contents—a post-human colony,
backs to the sun, waiting in a convoy
to move on into clearer air
after pollution warnings, dust-cloud hangovers,
jeep-crawling into the 23rd century.

Blacks and Grays

The high-end 21st century look:
William S Burroughs as its prototype,
the mapping YSL, Richard James, Hugo Boss,
like structural architecture
got into clothes
exec/casual black: exec/casual gray:
the a note in gray deepening colour
the black matte black stylistic gravity
suggesting ship's black paint
sans serif lettering done in spray bomb black,
black runny hair dye, Mafia conference tables,
the blackout in a gun barrel.
Gray's neutral and attracts colours
like purple, cerise, orange, red,
but finds a complementary line with black:
a locked in mood, a foggy quotient,
an emphasis more than a style
in composing attitude like menu
to fit with grainy emotion.
Take a black three-button blazer,
a gray cashmere jumper and charcoal slacks,
you have the 21st century future
like airport skies smudged at vanishing point
towards a global marker:
a texture that's backgrounded as a base
to building on like a Burroughs novel
as a lab-experiment, black and gray
by the canal today, the serious two,
cutting a deal and studiously dodgy
on the café patio in full view.

Dusty Springfield's (blues) at 5am

The voice is mink. The scent Trésor.
Dykes in the clandestine
1960s at Aubrey Walk—
she left her panda makeup on all night
so Sandra wouldn't see her stripped,
run-proof mascara like black dahlias
leaving no traces on the black pillow.
The ashtray's like a mortuary:
the bottle-green Booth's gin bottle bottomed-out
to a finger's width,
the uncapped Schweppes tonic bottle gone flat.
The room, (Anna Kavan's a street away),
smokes bluely—whitely, light tweaking
slatted Venetian blinds in mid-July,
light that mixes with the sleeping tablet's fog
into an opalescent 5am blur.
She sashays in a black silk negligée
into the bathroom's clinical sanctuary
to do full makeup before Sandra wakes,
the diva pop star lining eyeliner
like immaculate Chinese calligraphy.
She fires-up on the last clear lick of gin,
eyes squeezed on its hot corridor
into the gut, and then slinks back to bed.
Sandra's curled in a caterpillar shape,
black hair rayed out, the love bite on her neck
the colour of a blueberry.
Dusty feels flat, gravelly and wiped out.
She sits cushion-propped waiting for the day,
her mind configurating how she'll sing
a certain phrase—she scans it word by word—
lights up a fag for huskiness,
repairs her toe polish, while Sandra shifts
from dream to dream, face up, and stays that way.

My Lives

Thin. Looks like a pop star (high cheek bones
at low cloud level).
Owes all his poems to a pink jumper
(cerise, more raspberry),
seen on a bony shouldered man
at La Colette: popped juniper berries
mixing a tangy frisson with the sea,
one excerpted, truant, white-hazy afternoon,
a Thursday, circa 1973?
Clothes. Mostly a Mod aficionado:
the poems taking colour from a shirt
seen at the time, high collar button-down
blue gingham, (the tone unrepeatably
an offbeat deep blue subtext to navy) :
the wearer stepping into myth-making
as lyric building blocks to poetry.
Education. Hanging round, filling in
empty spaces with imagination.
Outsider, from those two teeny sightings,
a shirt and jumper obsessive
linking the singularity of each
to inspiration. Mods are detail-cute.
Occupation. Monitoring the crowd
for image, mostly in London's West End,
and working from it. Writing a poem's
like compressing the shattered galaxy
into a lively rectangle, 30 lines,
8 x 5? Biography: still unmixed
the unsettling secrets stored in the studio.
Agenda: getting the two colours right
a pink and blue that won't ever be matched,
but keep pointing up possibilities
of resolution on hazy Thursdays,
staring at futures, and eating ice cream
that's sharply, alertly dark raspberry.

It Takes Two Baby

Your ash-stained black fedora's rake
tilted back, slept-in, re-characterized,
a Johnson's of St James' punched
into a UFO shape, then the black shades
concealing 52 hours without sleep,
eye slants the colour of canned tomatoes
when the shades slip—
you hanging on the stairs
beneath a Vivienne Westwood poster
so large it hallucinates off the wall,
Sex in its snarlish punk World's End heyday
in 1976, SW3.
Two Marlboro Lites are sighting from your lips
with variant deposits of drooped ash
like flaky bullet heads,
an incendiary's burnt out bronchia—
40 a day, supplemented by cocaine.
You offer me the bottle of Pinot rosé
you're dragging on at 9.30 am:
wine the colour of a pink carnation.
I work the bookshop for you in a weird space-time,
me with my head speedy with poetry—
that's always my peculiar drug—
the dopamine acceleration of words
into such extravagant imagery.
We're broke. I tell you words are hot sapphires
if we could get an exchange rate—
a conversion into gratuitous Euros?
I've nothing in my coat but purple pens
and valium and space substituting for money.
A baguette's all I'll eat today
to fill the hunger. We embrace and stay
a minute folded in each other's loss
so that the contact hurts—it's come to this
a momentous event in which we bond
outside of the brutally sunlit indifferent day.

Going Down Slow

At first, I thought depression was like fog,
dispersible over an office tower,
a flaky vapour burnt off by pink sun
the colour of a red grapefruit,
but found its core was black and hard
and sometimes irreducible

the way an avocado stone
maintains obdurate guard
inside an egg plant's slippery leather skin.
I didn't know that it's interior
was subterranean like a corridor—
a mazy underpass with the lights blown

and menace graffiti-tagged on the walls.
I curled up there and notched myself
into a caterpillar's ball.
I had incentive, but I couldn't act,
and got so drunk glasses seemed redundant.
I drank relief clean out of the bottle,

corks littering the floor like dead bullets
a gutted war-zone in Baghdad.
I occupied a shrinking radius,
the TV on, and me reading it blank,
afraid if it grew silent I'd go mad
or end up drug-zonked in a hospital

orbiting pharmaceuticals
like friends I've visited who shook all day.
Letters accumulated in the hall—
unopened snow-drifts littering the floor.
I stayed inside and thought a black river
was waiting outside to break down the door.

Months of it, going down there, terminally?
No change of clothes, bunkered like the Führer,
the loaded pistol aching on his desk.
Half a stone dropped, not even poetry
worrying me into hyper-alert.
The blackness killed it in my chemistry.

No comfort, when the way up's the way down.
I wore black mirrored glasses everywhere
contactless as an alien
with an indifferent wraparound stare.
I scored some methadone by Centre Point
and tried to unplug pain. Nothing seemed real.

The nights were worst, the days like a dead train
derailed on a Siberian plateau.
I sat ten hours and didn't move at all,
convinced that losers win, got up at last
and took a pencil and wrote on plaster
like naming a new country on the wall.

We All Adore Johnny

Elusive, out of town again,
the blond-haired head-turner who stops our hearts
networks our conversation underground
in the 6pm Phoenix bar:
comparisons with a taller James Dean
or quiffed Billy Fury as prototype

brim on the tongue like strawberries
soaked in his favourite brand: Stolichnaya vodka
80 proof Russian bullet shot
stripping the lining from the throat.
I read us a Frank O'Hara poem
about the way a first vodka

triggers acceptance of almost anything,
like feeding emotions through a juicer.
Johnny's a vodka tearaway,
a dealer with a film-star's looks,
and by some freaky synchronicity
calls mid-conversation, so he's right there with us

as a connection in the bar
sustained by my Nokia signal.
He's heading north for three shape-shifting days,
no destination ever named,
he's somebody who perfects a dissolve
like fog worked to a blue consistency

on smoky blue: a seacoast texturing.
We order drinks and recreate his pull,
the hypnotic charm he asserts, the style—
his Valentino shades ledged in his hair,
the smile that's coloured banana-yellow,
his eyes the clear blue of a swimming pool.

We're like a fan club grouped into this bar
talking up Johnny and Frank O'Hara,
and how vodka is clear like poetry,
only its side effects are slightly skewed
and heady and hopefully off the wall
and burn like Johnny as a ruined star.

Thinking of JC (Good Times, Bad Times)

Back to the black railings on the meat-rack,
as pickupable skinny rent,
drugged attitude in eyeliner,
the big Grand Canyon dropdown—poverty
having you sell sex the Regent Street side
of Piccadilly: love for sale
with your wasted, broken body,
no punter aware of what lived in you
for good or bad, street poetry,
the helium lift of it like champagne fizz
poured as a gold sun in a scummy glass.
Propped up as damaged goods, your dignity
was lyric, a consolable re-run
of re-arranging the user and used
cased in a black T and pre-damaged jeans.
You sold yourself in alleys and hotels,
desperate to eat and write, feed a habit,
and somehow liberate a poetry
from degradation. You came out so ill
you never got back to the other side.
Today, the rich packing in Regent Street,
I'm reminded of your last stand, the day
somebody broke you and left you for dead,
and you crawled back to a friend's, gave it up,
but couldn't hate the man who'd beaten you,
and wrote a poem for him in your blood
that dried on paper to the darkest red.

Baby's Got a Gun

Sodium traces 0.2
these Chinese noodles are like super strings
I'll never count, but know exist,

a stir fry shuffle in the pan.
I don't remember books, only pop songs,
and this one like the singer's terminal.

Your bright pink T-shirt reads syntactically
Nobody Knows I'm A Lesbian.
The noodles twist like kiss curls on a fork.

Aliens

I meet them in the crowd. It's synchronicity
attracts, the way a stranger's eyes
connect, not orange or purple,
but silver, like they're pure neurology,
the recognition like the speed of light
travelling at 186,000 mph
per second: we're parallel worlders—
holographic inserts into reality,
but carbon-based: I tense, and find you out
and dissolve back into the saturated crowd.
That girl has a warp signature,
left-handed, left-sided, her shocking pink hair
translates into scarlet, then blacker roots.
She's come and gone, like tachyons, that fast
I think up the analogy—
an astronaut flying for five years at the speed of light
would re-enter the earth's atmosphere
to find five centuries had passed,
his body five years early, five years late.
I take my time out: the sky turns blue-green;
the moment's always loaded for contact,
searching irises, pupils, a facial type
in which the alien shows a split-second's
re-synchronised identity
in the gold light on Shaftesbury Avenue.
The sighting's personal: when the lights flip green
I cross the road, and hurry on my way
into dispersal, diffused in the crowd,
busy this side of nothing, hurrying
towards an open deadline with the day.

Prospecting Poet

A rogue gene infiltrating suits,
a thin cat versus the fat cat's
futures contracts, I work the line
parallel to the job I do,
sight it like a Boeing's fin flash
dipping through egg-whisked city cloud,

and jumpy with it all the day
in little spurts of chemical.
The man in my shop deals a drug
from the white gold rush, keeps it pinned
in dusty packeted rainbows,
to a re-sewn interior,

he's in the poem too.
I pick at bits like assembling a car
from parts, brake pads, cold air intake,
exhaust system, fuel tank, fuel pump
and keep it all as virtual stuff,
the poem's debris floating in my nerves.

Sara enters the poem blue
from an emotional break up,
steps into it, I keep writing
and note her hunted eye-corners
and edgy depleted energies
and how she's squashed down flat by recent hurt

like the lid on a Dart styrofoam cup,
the one beside me on the desk,
shaped like a logoed crop circle.
Rain on the windows looks like rhinestone snails
climbing a vertical glass plant.
The West End shimmers as smoky mirage.

I broker poetry like shares
on an imaginary Square Mile,
a notebook where nothing happens
but projection of metaphor
turned by this hand, while wet sunlight renews
its high-end spot gold index on the floor.

Current Affairs

Alan's Time

First hyacinths in the kitchen, violet cones
spilling to drop-dead gorgeous curls
in January, the day wearing 13
on a transparent slab of sky
that's champagne-coloured over Bedford Square
and blue-green over Sainsburys.
We talk of croc blood and it's 10.50.
Crocodile haemoglobin, rich in oxygen,
as answer for synthetic human blood,
a refrigerated freeze-dried powder
added to water?

                Alan's blue Levi's
have lost their indigo dye and their tone's
like the dusty veneer on blue car paint
collected from the motorway.
Our theme shifts to chickpea and chilli soup
and how its tetchy narcotic heat
raises metabolism like a snake.
The natural high's the chilli's capsaicin—
its defence against being eaten.
Alan has the residue from last night's
like a tropical sun in the saucepan.
Our redbrick façade fronts a library
where a girl sitting at a terminal
gets up and shakes a wing of violent hair
at 11.30. Her window's the blue lens
through which we name her Deborah
because she's Deborah-like. The phone collects
news from Bear River, Vancouver.
We're busy- busy and meet to slow time
to something malleable, and stand back from it
like a digital river. Who's closer
to death this moment I don't know; we move
there faster, slower, never parallel?

Deborah comes back from the stairwell. Her hair's
like hyacinths. The phone again:
Bear River confirmation Alan's house is safe:
(they're five hours back, we're five hours on)—
the rolling, muddy flood, he says,
driven by days of blinding rope-thick rain.

Opium for Men

I wear yours for our regular Fridays,
atomize dustings on my skin—
a YSL activator
tangy between us, top note held,
the shoulders of my black jumper.

Our ritual, and we've done it years—
at yours: 20 Holland Park Avenue,
the fig tree outside mopping up the light,
you both my friend and publisher
which seems to make it right?

Our habit, a decade of after-dinner sex
recombinant black cabs rushing outside,
Billie Holiday singing, 'He's funny that way,'
as we are, you in a Thai floral shirt
questioning if Paul Bowles was gay,

before we make it upstairs, leisurely,
a painting by Anna Kavan
staring us into noticing
the black-eyed junkie features, a sister
to her own habit—smack 3 times a day—

and it's the bedroom next, the pillows stacked
like London cumulus, the lamp
diffusing light like a hot peach,
obsessive order marked in everything—
your Tamazepam within easy reach,

the moment ours, and shelved around the room
the books you've published I first read
at 16/17, never thinking
I'd see them this way, Opium on my skin,
lying half-naked on your bed.

Back to Bill Franks

Big wide-screen movie clouds rolling over,
green, yellow and mauve slow chasers
clustering over Vauxhall Bridge—
the muddy churned tide turning on itself,
Jeffrey Archer's art-stashed penthouse upstairs,
his Warhol investments distressed
by a cryogenic market,
and we sit watching aquarium floaters,
red and black ruffle-finned fish do slo-mo
abrupt movements like edgy traffic lights
in a flat-screened aquarium.
I'm here to restructure your memories
as pointers to my sixties fashion book:
you as you were, things as they were
reinvented in the moment
like a cup-cake or macaroon.
The cars you drove: an Aston Martin DB5,
a gun silver Alfa Romeo sports,
turning the Aston over at Hyde Park Corner,
still transmit speed through your neural network,
real as the Carnaby Street that you owned,
tropical colours splashed in the windows,
the 1960s torrentially controversial
smart gender update: men as unisex.
We're comfortable together in pre-rain
indigo skyscape build, cloud skyscrapers
starting to peak, and me recording you
for fashion archive history maintain
our dialogue over chocolate biscuits,
dark bitter chocolate, as the rain comes on,
drivingly luminous, and the Archers
duck for their car with red golf umbrellas
big as two eruptive endgaming nuclear suns.

To a Friend in Despair

Your marriage shattered like a car windscreen,
the debris littering your Meard Street flat,
   the rows so vicious, words came out
   you'd never used before, their hurt
rivalled by hers, as though she'd learnt to shout
spontaneously from you: your leather hat
lending a Colony Rooms gangster air

to years of dissipation, so acute
you drank quadruple vodkas through the night
   blinded into lucidity
   at 4am by a visionary light
rayed out inside you from another gram
cut on a jewel case—molecular rocks
coking your bloodstream, powdering your suit,

the dawn erupting in the Soho sky,
your wife listening with dread for your return,
   an entourage of hangers on
   still anxious to do lines and burn
defiantly, despite the breaking day.
The music rocked the windows like a blast
shaking the flat with panicky reverb,

before the row exploded, Tiggy up,
hands angularly positioned on her hips,
   the throw outs scattering downstairs
   and you the fall man in a suit with rips,
a lacerated Westwood grey chalk stripe,
found it a game, until things grew perverse,
your disappearances more regular,

your slow immersion in the underworld
demanding callousness and secrecy,
   you somewhere on a pop star's floor

   passed out from drugs—hash, Ecstasy,
revived at dawn by vodka, a red sun
poured in the glass to liberate a mood
black as a stairwell—and the morning gone

in a redundant sleep, before the pub
mid-afternoon, the French House on Dean Street,
   recharged you with gunned vodka shots,
   their glacial chill imparting heat
to your slurred brainfade, your bravado pitched
into the raw indifferent company
like action-painting over desperate

negotiations with an inner pain
you kept dark like an underground river,
   the one tracking under your street
   sluicing poisons like your liver.
You got to know your precinct, each crack den,
each drinking club, before she threw you out
repeatedly in a cyclonic rage

and still you'd crawl back home abstemiously
to be reprieved—I'd get you one more chance
   arguing your case the next day
   against a hostile stonewall diffidence,
the woman in her office hyping power
as an assault on sensitivity
every cell wired to make the client pay

optimally for Helmut Newton shoots . . .
You blew it all, one final time, Kate Moss
   leading you up the powder trail
   and only sobered to your loss,
as something final, the locks changed, the voice
frozen at minus zero, no least give
in its closure on all emotional roots,

the tone so hard, the hurt was physical.
Your fall accelerated, now that hurt
   alerted you like lemon juice
   to everything in her you'd miss
and took for granted, and the night became
continuous—a Soho corridor,
you working it, no longer as a game,

but as a means to blanking like a wall
at what you'd done—destroyed a life
   and with it yours, your loneliness
   turning in you like a sharp knife
each time the drug wore off, reality
burning the window as violet sunlight

and used your phone frantically like a gun
to offer reparation and were met
   predictably with a renewed hostility,
   her truculence converting your regret
into an anger that was never meant
but mixed with hers was like a fireball
terrorists had ignited in the street.

Depression followed as a blackout phase
submerged in you like a sunk mooring rope.
   You couldn't work or deal in books
or pay the bills stacked high- rise in the shop
but got up late afternoon and half dead
came in and pocketed whatever cash
would feed a habit that you couldn't stop.

The damage grew until we couldn't reach
you for the lies, and now you turn away
   from everything familiar you knew,
   as though you want the world to pay

for what you've lost, but still I see a light
burn in you like it's locked inside a safe,
constant, untouched, because it's really you.

What the Dead Do

Bill's red carpet-red sofa's a benchmark
for blue, or a hangover's dispersal
looking out at Albert Bridge,
the river tracking in combats
and jumpy sudoku plots to Vauxhall,
our sci-fi breakfast Miso tubed

on blue poppy seed crackers topped
with blueberries nutritionally packaged
for fat-free optimal zip energies
works on the taste with saliva stick-shift.
A London day's like a movie premier
across the river—acute happenings—

an orange sunburst shattering the haze,
so many individual lives focused
on intensely separate realities,
no common centre, only sex and tea
and watching out for menace on the street
in our oppressive anonymity.

There's no shared time, Bill scans the stock market's
irregularities: I'm tight with time
converting it into word imagery
on his red sofa, that's my point in space,
an 8x4 dimension occupied
back of Whitehall and East of Waterloo,

the sky changing from muzzy gray to blue
as an adventure. Something's in the air,
a stimulus like vitamins, a gene
having me imagine what the dead do,
both in and outside me: Bill's lost between
possible slumps and the obituaries,

and how the light's increased inside the flat
to pineapple, an orange that's not gold,
but yellow measured in glow on the floor
that dusts the sofa gold lame, while Bill
busies himself with major indices
and plans to catch himself before a fall.

Dylanologist

He wears UV blocking aviators,
ex-pilot's from an aircraft auction,
his aviation memorabilia
incorporating Convair-B58 Hustler
fundamental cockpit fixtures.
He's an obsessive bootleg Dylanologist,
 wearing anti-sun shades even indoors.
The bathroom's a black marble mausoleum,
prints of the man mounted strategically,
indomitable black shades, springy curls,
a smudge of taciturn mystique
circa the Rolling Thunder Revue tour . . .
The cabin features are a distraction,
old BA ashtrays, a flying jacket
warped like a rhino's skin, a flight manual.
He works on the definitive discography,
(bootlegs included). His Sara
is Alice: green eyes big as tennis balls,
lips ovalled to red elasticity,
her presence an obsessive enigma.
He keeps throwing switches on rarities,
a light bulb moment rehearsal track, canned demo.
He drapes the flying jacket. Alice broods.
He's found an early swipe at 'Love Minus Zero.'

e-mailing Edmund White

I click to open yours: the thunder rain
outside, accelerating without brakes,
a ripping flash-flood in fatigues,
khaki and green, the ante on the spine
finned with orange September leaves,
a torrential debacle grooving my street
at 4pm, me splashing back
in black size 7 Converse All Star baseball boots
to read your latest in our shared anthology
of writing secrets: Paxil, three heart drugs
regulating your chemistry,
your weight up again, like an office tower
of hydrogenated fats—you worry
the lights will go from an exploding fuse
mid-sentence, a blown artery,
a gasket detonating in your heart.
We're honorary French: our preferences
confected from their literature—
the poet as flaneur, his imagery
like skylights picking out in a silk shirt
a blotched defiant stain. The violent shower
increases—I've opened the garden door
for atmospherics, and poppies are thrashed
to pink and red confetti. Time, you say,
that's optimal is measured out in words,
the rest is filler. You're tented in bed,
a laptop platformed on your knees—
autumn in New York, your weekend reprieve
from Princeton tutorials, the village light
the colour of a maintained blonde?
I click and send like stun gunning your brain,
worry about my overloaded nerves
that feel like depleted tube track,
and listen out and find a calmness in
the busy dialogue of dazzling rain.

Book Catalogue

Rain, and the sound's like reading Baudelaire
on empty Sundays. No 260
'SHAKESPEARE, William. The Sonnets. CUP—
(1966), rpt. 1981. Wrps. 274 pp.
Derek Jarman's heavily annotated working copy . . .'
punctuating domestic agendas:
my neighbour sits watching Godard
in a white studio, gentian T-shirt,
her face a pink carnation with red lips.
I watch her like a movie, push her hair
to platinum sculptures, then pour it back.
'Used in preparation for "The Angelic Conversation"
(1985), his film based on Shakespeare's sonnets.
In this preliminary selection . . .'
Rain nurtures my potted fritillaries,
and revives memories of clueless Sundays
in Amsterdam's American Hotel
spent reading Baudelaire to reprised rain:
me shaking from withdrawal: the harbour in the sky.
'The film maker's made annotations in two different
colour inks alongside on 22 pages,
varying from a simple asterisk
to suggestions . . .'   I play the Coil soundtrack,
and watch the rain pull out. My snake-headed
fritillaries have purple python skin:
my neighbour's doing costume changes for the mirror.
A diluted orange sun
fires up my decision to buy the book,
signed "for Coil Derek Jarman
Phoenix House December 1981."

Somewhere a Change

The garden's pumpkin-coloured overnight;
September/October: a scarlet slash
of nasturtiums: a red striptease.
I play Dylan's scoping Blood On The Tracks
as blues panacea to arrest hurt,
his lifeline hooky 'Tangled Up In Blue'
meeting me as upbeat itinerary

on days when twinkling showers interpret
a pattern on skinny-ribbed orange leaves.
You left me, and I never got it back
the life I've lost, buried like an old knife
eroded in the ground, blunt in a tree,
or just discarded in the pyramidal ephemera
of things that never make it composite
again, like damage caused by shot-down love
that squeezes like a clenched fist in the heart.
It turns me over like a planet's spin,
shakes me out like trouser pockets searched through
before the cleaners; and the leaves are down,
blood-orange red, canary, black and green,
shaken out of a blotchy crown,
and I'm insomniac, up half the night,
afraid of what my dreams reveal, and sitting there,
islanded by the white pool of a reading light.

Current Affairs

The headache in my hypothalamus
persists like weather, isobars
of pressure—Paracetamol,
Nurofen or Aspirin dissolve?—
it's deep space location, a fist

impacted in grey matter.
I review its neural website,
attack with 2x
300mgs, and visualize
the pain as like a mushroom cloud

sited above a nuked warehouse
or like a mini-Battersea
power station chipped as an implant
into an apple core.
My black jacket's a Kenzo; the logo

maintains my balance, doing tricks
with my aesthetic, like a patch
worn on the skin to alter chemistry.
The sky over the harbour's green,
a menthol slash/peppermint

and above Shell refineries
a blue more lapis lazuli
than French: a longing for blue love
that atomizes into sea.
My headache shifts from red alert

to grainy vision. I stand back
to back with a yard off Victoria Pier.
The traffic loops inside my head.
The day smells clean as a grapefruit.
The light checks in and comes up clear.

Rewriting Shakespeare's Sonnets

A czar's bombproof bunker's solidity,
you thought those 14-liner rectangles
power-locked like a black Jag's doors,
cryopreserved by centuries
like a vitrified organ
cooled below 120° C.
A Tudor troubleshooting exercise—
he fucked his wife over the kitchen chair
between 138–139,
no corrections, just tactical chutzpah,
ripe venison for breakfast, booze all day
and the line clean as skyscraper architecture
solid as a moon mountain
a Wall Street investment in bisexuality—
a black woman and a rent boy for the two
operatives in his knotty liaison
he wrote out in reflective hours
chilling from dodgy property crunches,
power-lunches with spotty quangos,
listening to rain or watching a pink rose
open to a ruched detailed tumbling scent.
The poet and the criminal
locked like an iPod in a Ziploc bag,
they're inseparable and the rewrite needs
a mix as potent—break the code
and reconvert, get gunned down for the try,
listening to Boeings bisect the city sky.

You Wear It So Well

A black hat on the night's excess,
worn like the tricky rock dodger Pete Doherty,
a scarlet shirt slashed open, mid-torso,
you're space-walking mid-afternoon
still trying to connect through disconnect,
cocaine and alcohol trafficking
metabolites through your tired blood.
I feel for you, rooting amongst exhausted shirts,
Brooks Brothers, Ben Shermans, for a clean one
that holds its shape, a John Pearse stitched jacket,
(you've worn the same clothes for three days),
their fatigue mapped by rips and stains,
and can't remember where you slept,
Soho, or a parallel universe,
the music loud as sonic chemistry,
the sex if it happened, fantasy stuff,
like fucking in weak gravity,
you don't remember, now uploading porn
to recreate the stimulus
as a grainy brainfaded residue.
I help you readjust, and buy you food,
a tahini and chilli falafel,
something to earth you after moon-walking
through nights and days that have no barriers
but flip into dissolve. Sometimes you see
in colours, sometimes black and white,
according to the substance. You're down there,
and I'm down there, meeting in a basement.
I collect a polythene bag of pills,
but we talk books, and Thom Gunn's poetry,
and live the moment for the odd, bizarre
makings it has of a timeless event.

CHINA YUM YUM

Jaffa Cakes

It mattered outside—pink hydrangeas—
a lipstick pink bleeding to mauve and blue
pumped up by iron, like steroids,
and that your black iPod was branded Zen,
a compact Chinese alien
loaded with Turkish pop, and that the day
was Sunday in the rubber universe
and that we sat out back before the rain
banking ideas—I want to be
an image banker, selling corporates
access to colouring facts with imagery,
giving thought-patterns notes, contours,
an individual edge, a quantum leap
out of the grey room into blue
oxygenated imaginative reality.
And Jaffa cakes, it mattered too
you chose the third and fifth selectively
by looking to negotiate
a symmetry, 38mm
chocolate layered over orange jelly,
54mm diameter,
1 gm of fat—I need the specifics
of this McVitie's masterpiece,
a slim-line bite we crunch by scaffolding,
you telling me that the Black Sea's
a deep turquoise—I choose the first and last
as my endgaming do or die
thee-layered tangy sponge finality.

Kitchen Poem

The tea cupboard's 90% Lapsang Souchong,
Higgins, Harrods, a tea-snob nose
for the smokiest bonfire brew
leaves crackly as gravel crunched underfoot.
I keep a mint Cape Goliard copy
of J. H. Prynne's *Kitchen Poems*
copyright 1969
obscure as a Russian menu
beside the tea for its complexity.
Most of my thinking happens there,
lateral, intuitive, the flashes
like a choice of brand marmalade
red as the defining moments in a redhead's hair.

The Difference between Harrods' and Fortnum's Smoky Teas

Straight through the Luxury Room's Cartier glitz,
the Food Hall's marble mausoleum's submerged light's
my point of focus here, for teas that smell
like wisteria simmering on a wall,
pressed by the sun like a lavender shirt,
hung out to dry. I know the canisters
and the smoky exhalation
brimming from favourites like China White Point's
extravagant depth; a gunpowder scent
spiked with a bonfire's cooked embers,
to Tarry Souchong's tunnel-notes
fuming with subterranean promise,
or upgrade to the jasmine flowers
modifying compressed Lapsang
in summery Imperial Gold.
                                      300 gms of each,
the same of an obdurate Lapsang Souchong,
smelling of 1950s lived-in car leather:
my expectation massaging the tongue.

From the speeded-up Knightsbridge congestion
choking with foot traffic to Piccadilly
and Fortnum's tea tins blocked in high- rise cubes
five storeys—Russian Caravan—
(too retarded in density):
I pick a whiffy Earl Grey, Lapsang inflected,
and a clean Lapsang coloured by Earl Grey
as note-happy interchanges
of mid-tempo meditative teas,
the kind that provoke reflective debate
with little fish-tailed memories.

My dark green bulky Harrods tea packets
crackle if knuckled with pressure,

smoke in the morning like mist on a stream,
the big leaves wriggling like tadpoles
in amber. They're for complex states,
Fortnum's for lighter mid-afternoon moods,
Harrods for deeper underworld traffic,
sat in the kitchen modifying brews
by honey pots and a jar spilling red nasturtiums.

China Yum Yum

My Oolong leaf tea wiggles in the pot
the leaves attempting weak handclasps
in their chaotic dispersal
like a truncheon rebuffed riot
hissy with steam, my morning ritual
the sky outside like lipstick bleed
slashed on upended charcoal blocks.
I slant Ines' cute leopard-print hat
top of a shirt pile, as the one she wears
at St Martin's Central, her eyes made up
navy blue as a thunder sky.
China she says is bigger than the moon
if you're an individual in its mass,
a name going for a blood test
in a body shopping economy
of organ traffic. The world's mostly parts,
genital tissue in lip collagen,
alien egg donors. When my tea comes up
it tastes of China on a rainy day
in hills building steadily into cloud.
Ines is in her orange flat
razoring cuttings from style magazines
into a collage assemblage
of cartoonish visual hits. She gets fat
because she needs to fill space in
and be an island. I stay thin
to match the mad accelerated times.
I pour my tea out like a song.
A Chinese cargo ship from Guangzhou
steams towards Durban racked with arms
to be refused entry. The day breaks blue
like surf over a roof: my tea builds notes
from Chinese molecules and Ines calls
full of the hat she's making and her art
littered with sequins, feathers, pins and glue.

First Out

The atmosphere's a sunny upbeat beach,
euphoric tropics even in winter
in our small café on St Giles High Street,
I need that place like a familiar key
stabbed in my door, as the serrations grip.
Two wooden floors, and both a gallery

for the iconically camp: Liz Taylor
as Cleopatra, indigo makeup
overblown by Alberto de Rossi,
James Dean, explosively lean biker boy
worrying acute pain into his look,
Marlene, Bette and Shirley Bassey,

confected into lipstick overkill
by how the artist worked that focal point
into a strawberry-shaped identity.
It's like a charcoal painted ship lit up
behind Centre Point, a bar below deck
sanctioned for the DJ's dance-beat attack

on Saturdays, but mostly the soundtrack
fits with the hour, relaxed, moody, sexy,
grainy or soul-broody mahogany,
we move with it, four seasons in a day
textured into the easy ambience
in which the undecided and the gay

share little details, just like calories
observed in dieting. I dip into
the early evening there, the happy hour,
the sky outside like a blue square cut tie,
a drink—a first one—rounding out edges,
the city shifting gear, I feel the roar

of get away accelerate across
its concrete diaphragm and find refuge
in a window seat, I can see from there
the lives I'll never know of passersby
like grainy footage, and sometimes a pink
rip of red sunset in the evening sky.

Thundery Blues

A navy-blue donut of compressed cloud
hangs on the city WC2—
SW1, a blue hydrangea head
like bio-war terror
leaked out of Africa, a Congo lab.
I go outside, and you walk into me
after five years, Alex in black
back from the south, dancing tango, cancan
in teasy violet feathers, each high kick
she gestures, scorching like the sirocco.
Alexandra's like a mantra
coded into my breath, she taught me chant
to liberate the snake in me,
a kundalini tingle in the spine.
The clouds remind me of packed blueberries
I buy at M&S, a dusty indigo
more black than blue. Alex's coffee tan
brings sunlight stored in her pigment
into the street and tangy pine
and zingy pheromones, as though she's been
coming to meet me for five years
in a moment's spontaneous synchronicity
shared outside under rumbling steamy skies
black as an oyster imagines the sea.

Sooner or Later Frank

You end up listening to his quotient
  of rainy day, blue-mooded songs,
Sinatra sounding like he's in a bar
  by drizzly New York docks, the voice
a lived-in confidential baritone
  that always seems familiar,
bourbon-shot, 2am reminiscent,
  resigned, resistant to the hurt
he phrases neutrally, for bashed about
  means changing partners like a shirt,
a red and white striped Brooks Brothers affair,
  the tie dropped like a hanging man,
the attitude an emotional outlaw
  who never gets the answers right
and talks them into blue and indigo
  inflections, gangsterish felt hat
angled defiantly, tipped north or south
  for studio or mafia wear
and always integral to the Frank look
  that's in the voice: he's right in life,
so centred in it, he's like a peach stone
  pivotal to brimming texture,
but at the same time sitting in alone
  on loneliness, an Alka Seltzer glass
fizzing to opalescence in his hand,
  the woman gone, her Chanel scent
left as a fuzzy hangover. It's loss
  he builds on and converts to gain,
but still it's trouble, win or lose, and both
  feed into song—the ones you hear—
his pick-up fuming, just a casual bit,
  her lipstick bleeding on a coffee cup,
downtown, while he sits sorting out his socks,
  to the soundtrack of steady New York rain.

Listening to Johnnie Ray in Bed, Baby

The night comes on amplifying fridge sounds
bottles mostly—white Pinot Grigio,
Martini and square-shouldered Gordon's Gin
in a frosty green gangster suit:
my unstoppable need to drink sustained
by how its curve links into poetry

late night, the quiet between 12 and 1
as optimal resources to my stab
at giving words a Kitkat crunch, a swing
like Johnnie Ray's colouring of a phrase
from blue to unexpected high end pink
that keeps on stretching to a hot cerise

emotional marker, then dips back to blue,
textured by slangy orange, middle grey
for the dejected part on 'All of Me,'
or rawer, hot from his explosive core,
in pulpy mango colours, like he bruised
each note in finding that it really hurt

to pitch a song with the intensity
of 'Cry,' the awkward masculinity
alert to lapses in its guard—Johnnie
mauled by the law for same-sex offences,
broken for being gay and put on ice,
his chain of hits smashed by reputation,

Johnnie who drank like emptying a lake
to piece himself together, partied hard
by black swimming pools on Mulholland Drive,
downed magnums, flipped over a red Cadillac,
but came back always, skewed and deaf on stage,
missing the beat and crowding the song

with bougainvillea gestures, comes at me,
writing in bed at 1 a.m.—full-on
from a big 1950s microphone
(unknotted blue tie and unbuttoned shirt)
giving it all one foggy summer's day,
sweaty, uptight and brutally alone.

Dorian Gray: the Physicals

Bevelled grey boards, ten butterfly designs
stamped in gilt, Ward, Locke & Co 1891,
an orange neon sun
120 years on
comes up, we're eating cinnamon-and-rice ice cream
from Lazio on Wells Street
dilapidated pagoda turrets:
and the spoon jumps—250 numbered copies
on Van Gelder handmade paper
signed by Wilde (for Dorian)
you know the antipodean shift again
zoning to dot and rib spiral condoms
for come-velocity and pak choi
M&S seal 3 like a condom pack.
Title page, half title by Charles Ricketts,
three-quarters vellum gilt—
Wilde gave his copies out to Dilly rent
who sold on, what you do you do
and it don't alter, like this line I write
as a commitment, and Wilde never said
if Dorian's eyes were green or grey or blue.

Grey Eyes

Your grey eyes, they're a foggy day,
two opalescent misty twists
pigmenting iris, red contrails
like sunlight mixed in a fuzzy vapour
over a harbour's whiteout
Agnieszka:
your name's four syllables going deep space
in memory, like a password
to what's behind the grey:
the you stretched out across your thoughts
like sky that lacks an end
to its grey tracking.
We meet over a photo
of someone (you?) escaping its edges
to an imaginary space you conceived,
we both see differently.
The white Sauvignon frees us up
to talk roots, yours a knobby walnut tree
on a Polish farm, mine a potato,
the pitted, moony, Jersey pedigree
cooked surface slippery as a pearl.
Our blood's got city-mapped, its direction
like the Circle line, involved
in London findings, tunnelled dark
and out to light, and back again,
like life forced through the arteries.
Your photo though, a black and white
enigmatic face like a dice,
a tennis ball got powder-licked,
an off-human tilted ovoid,
comes up between us—laid down flat,
and when your grey eyes lift away
I'm in their colour like resistant fog.

Pop

Pop

It's the soundtrack to our lives
an inherited poppy gene
not helical but Elvis-shaped
iconic DNA,
a new post-1950s strand
responsive each time we hear
a modern flavour in a voice
or edgy uptake of a band
inheriting collective pop
as a modified signature
and washing colours in the mix
a blue, an urban grey or pink,
and coming on as a blood-cleansing
fidgety stimulus, a hook
like an addictive sonic drug
I can't let go all day
deposited in my tune-bank
as banditry, a riff
provoking dopamine,
four-bars locked in my neural
circuitry that worry in
and stay
linked to my personality
as what it means to be alive
inside a mood-themed song
brightening big city air
for 2 or 3
colour saturated minutes
of transient wonder
that for the moment's permanent
as anything I'll get
popping in my cells
as a big and little
sweet and sad flavoured event.

Lolita

It wasn't the hip-hemmed babydoll
in see-through lipstick pink
or the glossy scarlet toes
peeping through toe-less stilettos
or the insolent moody look
too lived-in ever to wipe out—

a petulant disclaimer
of grungy motel sex
or the way she bobbed her hair
like a French film noir movie star
or licked her lips for dusting
on a jam-wedged donut

or kept to herself like Russia
a land mass apart,
lazy with fizzy hormones
and a mouth shaped like a heart,
or the trust fund she leeched
as an offshore asset,

like a diamond tooth
grainy with caviar.
But Lol had a secret
an Alka-Seltzer rocket
1cm water
in a film canister

placed upside down,
the tablet effervescing
into explosive force,
the trick done in a mini
with bunchy tartan pleats
to launch the catapult.

Lol sucked an index fingernail
like a cassis-tipped lollipop
a fangirl physicist
in a home-studio lab
launching a seltzer rocket
labelled Cease to Exist.

Japanese French

Burberry mac and the omelette
a global mix.
The pop's English ubiquity

like sushi in the wrong country
tangy, but without flavour.
Her orange and blue striped T-shirt update's

like Venetian blinds closed on her torso.
French pop's a linguistic misfit
like speaking with a mouthful of noodles,

she knows that now by the Bastille
arrondissement XIe XIIe,
and how the men look at her back to front

if she's in dusted skinny jeans,
a denim twist like a corkscrew
low rise pencil leg Miss Sixty

rivets and sanserif lettered logo
as eye candy detail
like a leather industrial plate.

The omelette's too greasy,
too unmalleably sticky, spiked with cheese
it tastes like a broody attic.

It's the river draws her,
lapidary infected green, managing
the city like its consciousness.

She's happy solo in the square,
pop as her accompaniment,
the omelette rejected like post mortem,

her Burberry lined with tartan,
the traffic going one way, she the other
towards a hissy steam-clean hotel-slippery shower.

Moving On

I want the video in front of earth
International Space Station blue
best unpolluted unobstructed blue
view in the stratosphere.
My shopping list, I lost it in the shop,
marinated artichoke hearts,
chocolate-chip cookies, and moved on,
the list like a found poem scored in red
asterisks, another star-belt
on paper, not a gaseous Big Bang.
I rewrite shopping lists as poetry,
the speed of life accelerating through
my blood as stardust energies,
the drive bumping up my capillaries
in Waitrose, Planet Organic or Boots,
the age in me like colour in a wine
inside the skin. I'm taken by beach balls
on the red planet Mars, plastic rovers
inflated with xenon gas
from Angström Aerospace in Uppsala,
sensors and cameras in a tough condom.
I move with that—a Mars survey gizmo
written up in New Scientist:
the blue sky bluer after checkout-point
the carrier leaving track marks on my wrist.

Missing You

It's always the same pull at 6pm
a gravitational jolt alert
like a jumpy air-pocket
Wakako Sakata
to our familiar edgy meeting place
the Foyles entrance on Charing Cross Road
you maintaining a pavement niche
under the red sans-serif sign
scrolling your cell-phone like a cyber pet
a pink networking alien
your red retro Dior eyewear
a winner with gold sequinned beret,
your boots two olive-green statements
fringed at the knee,
the Purple Magazine inside your bag
heavy as industry.
Today I found a paint-blotchy paper plane
crashed in the street, red white and blue
wing markings slashed with the word Help,
and written on the fuselage, I've crashed,
and looked up at the block above
searching for an open window, a sign
of someone's desperation, a kidnap
at 6pm, our time, and needed you,
the street smeared with white noise and Foyles nearby,
its time-warped quirky neon sign
a fried tomato red and walked on by
remembering our random game of naming clouds
tracking in patterns through the rolling city sky

Saint Jamie

You in your punky self-designed T-shirts—
Vanity, Poverty, Revenge,
Reichstag graffiti fonts
blocked onto queer icons
bike from Islington to Soho
on an aluminium frame
a streamlined savvy weapon
below a silver kilogram
routing through hydrocarbons
a Nikon in your bag,
the kindness in your deep-seat hurt
always breaking me up.
You're solid in my need
as a black Beckstein grand
an impulsive emotional give
deep as a book I've read
and buried in my nerves.
Your eyes are blue sky carriers
your look spins me round
 spookily off-world New Zealand
sunk in you like a fish-spine
the rub of soft and gritty streetwise
coming up in your shine.
We meet like that: your butch photos
fronting GQ and Boyz:
my poems burning in my veins
like scorched tyre treads,
I'm ill this week and your support
seems like a molecular column,
a 6 ft emotional rainbow
that doesn't vaporize.
Trust for me's St Jamie,
in my vulnerability,
you as my riffy bad boy avenger
putting an edgy trouble right,

then firing off to photo-shoot a star
gobbled up by makeup and botox
in a lowlight Soho bar.

London/Tokyo

A rainy, churned up, egg-whisked Soho sky
at 6 pm, Charing Cross Road
a mini-Tokyo
of Japanese redheads in skinny jeans,
die-cast hollow metal ipods
licked black or glossy raspberry,
fangirls in minis on Old Compton Street,
a cat-faced species, as I go
to meet
Toyoko at Piccadilly, her fringe
redone to a red frozen waterfall
I like to flick for paintbrush density.
The evening comes on with the sonic roar
of big-city white noise, a shattering
like the Heathrow corridor
compressed into Shaftesbury Avenue.
I bring her candy pink sweetpeas,
a poem as bits in my head,
and a 230 rococo violet chocolate bar,
an indigo pansy on the wrapper,
and all my past mixed in my chemistry,
molecularised as history,
she doesn't know and can't make real.
A black cab's diesel blasts into my face,
my excitement spikes up, I'm nearly there,
some mashed red sky over the Haymarket
just one tone redder than Toyoko's hair.

Hot and Cold

The summer's all shook up like a cocktail,
edgy clouds, revving isobars,
the sun cold as an amber traffic light,
shut out, endgaming through the haze
like frozen orange juice.
I do my day by opening out
to catches in the light, freed up
by the surprises—Lisa's call
from Grande Arroyo CA—
6,000 thunder hits smashing her night,
her bedroom slashed by hot lightning, each pull
a stomach-punch, it rocked her so
she tented under the duvet 6 hours
then went outside to humming birds and air
so ionised, it seemed to burn her skin
and stay there, sniffy, booting up
a shattered cosmic window, a blue hologram
of final things in formation.
I tell a friend that Elvis' last meal
was ice cream cones and chocolate-chip cookies,
information I keep in me
like kiwi smoothies in a fridge.
I wear a black wool blazer in August,
a snippet to resist a chill
so particled with dust,
it feels a raw no-season, a grey slab
of hot and cold delivered to my blood
this East side out from Lisa London day
burning with traffic like a power-chord.

Billy Fury

Two hours spent choreographing a gelled quiff—
the strands notable as teeny
calligraphy,
forelock collapsed like a question mark,
a decorative tearjerker's C,

a trichologist's inventive trompe l'oeil.
The jacket's molten gold mohair,
gold as bath taps in the Chateau Marmont.
He's scouse, from foggy Mersyside,
dreaming of gateways opening in the mist,

a way of life beyond warehouses, docks,
the sluggish grey of muddy fishtailed tides:
the sensitive one with a leaky valve
and degenerative arteries
ferried in and out of A&E,

a hole in the heart redder than the sun.
The odd one, shy one, trapped by shop windows
into awareness of his difference,
buying his mother roses on Sundays,
and risking neighbourhood threat for the looks

accompanying his extravagantly outlawed gesture.
Fame was a local thing, then endemic,
the crooner breaking every teenage heart
with his dejected air of irreparable loss
no girl could recompense or ever half repair,

his photo posters pinned on bedroom walls,
dripping with attitude and loneliness
and just a hint of availability,
his smile a dark blue rainbow acceding
to a bright twist of hope, a honeyed lick

of conceding to a perfect stranger
Billy the heartbreaker in blue lamé,
inflecting love-hearts into every song
on Radio Luxembourg, then losing out,
his music obsolete, his veins collapsed

from fatty myocardial furring,
spending time watching birds on a Surrey farm,
a yellow wagtail, buzzard, a bullfinch,
a paint-box of finches, or biking through the hills
aware of his mortality like fuel

injected in the red streamlined Honda,
dying in the fast-lane at 43,
snow like pink sugar dusting on the hills,
a jay grabbing for nuts, and round him spring
regenerative with spiky red-eyed daffodils.

Something the Matter

I'd slept the rain out like amnesia—
3 poppies dressed by Alexander McQueen
were de-clued of scarlet petals,

red silks littered my siesta,
the CD reprogrammed to zero,
I'd blanked 10 tracks, gone dead on Dylan's last,

the missing time documenting water,
a green pool outside showing limpid cool
the colour of a bamboo.

The rain was up there in cloud confection.
I fine-tuned info in my nerves
about the lateral shift, the disconnect,

low blood sugar. My voicemail saved
your message left in real time—1.30:
your tone like disembodied poetics

retrieved at 2pm.
I'd read of quarks clustering to create
protons and neutrons in every atom,

but couldn't picture their reality.
The book I'd been reading was shut
like declassified papers.

I reconnected with the afternoon,
made tea, built sound through the speakers,
busied myself in the purple kitchen

getting ahead, the torrential rain back
stripping the garden's flashy silks and me
flipping a moon-shaped Aspirin in a glass.

Sisters

Their kiss shapes the sound Copacabana—
bobbed Otoa in a mini (dahling)
and triangular-faced Parisian
red lipsticked Laura
hot on each other like a toffee stick
in this gender-flexi bar
with veggie culinary delectations
popping like hailstones to the taste.
I bring in my own variant of time,
dystopian signals travelling in my blood
like cellular traffic—the city haze
caught on my coat as fuzzy hydrocarbons.
Sisters feed on the music
spiked with euphoria like a push up bra.
I read the latest QX, Boyz,
no real advance in politics, no (?)—
give in straight hegemony, (no?)—
light in seeing round the bend
an altered state defiant end.

London My Time

It's like a planet cooking in blue gas,
fine particles (PM10),
an urban sprawl like a black omelette
scraped off the deep fry pan.
Gabby does falafel the best,
a size 4 shoe-wedge, a pitta-

wrap like a cala
lily's throat
with a gherkin hatpin.
Sometime's London's like a sunk continent
I lift out of REM sleep
into a pixellated reality,

its landmarks projected like Boeing fins
above the carbon soup,
the sun an orange lollipop
over frog-coloured Waterloo,
the river sluggish as a slow
sludgy bayou.

I meet Johnny on Ganton Street
off Carnaby, our reason shirts
at Sherry's, paisley button-downs
and rainy turquoise stripes on black,
crisp cotton toys
for style-conscious London boys,

city adoptees by default,
West enders, stickers to safe territory.
East I remember yards, a pub
in drizzly, edgy Leather Lane,
my publisher drinking a glass mountain
of Becks in there, and ripping off

his writers like slashing a tyre.
North, south, are like a long haul flight
from central, they're parallel zones
reached by the tube's volcanic roar,
cranky, loopy, underground track
patched up like a triple bypass.

Stand anywhere, and my feet move
independently from the speed
locked in the pavement's groove.
Crossing you need a cabby's memory
to get you to the other side:
slabs, skyscrapers, dodgy gated estates,

a khaki collar point of muddy tide.
I keep my concrete patch today,
track the square mile across Soho
meeting life in the only way
full-on, a year compacted in a minute
accelerated to vanishing point.

Summer in the City

Four Amazonian lilies detonate,
testicular roots packed into bashed pots
a steamy hot pink pungent scent attack
that's sauna tropical.
June fogs up with big city cloud
like hydrogen soup before the Big Bang.
The love bite I've placed on Toyoko's skin
deepens to true blue indigo
the colour of a blueberry
an island mapped out like Madagascar.
Sweet peas loop rainbows round a wiry vine.
The sunlight dusts my jeans like a runway
open to the queue of 727s
in the white noise white heat mid-afternoon.
My best friend cracks under his loss
that's like the weight of Africa.
He drinks himself into a bottle
of alcoholic blood without a glass.
I tire from writing like I've run across
a continent looking for my lost shoes.
A piloting bee crash-lands in the grass.
I phone my friend, sit on bare wooden boards
to speak, licked over with black paint.
The heat's grainy as orange juice
mixed into the day's scorched anthology
of small events, none bigger than the opening
of an explosive shocking pink lily.

MOON GANGS

E. Coli

It builds luxurious culture in the petri dish,
gut flora like a choked up rain forest
busy with toucans, jacamars,
monarch butterflies and red tanagers,
evolving E. coli populations
network metabolic pathways
of microbes, each inheriting a tail
dropped like a lizard in the passing on
rammed as rush hour Tokyo,
each cell's individual tempo fine-tuned
as a guitar figure, a riff
become the soundtrack to the times,
ringing chords tooled to angles and contours.
I feed my gut pre and probiotics
4 billion friendly bacteria per capsule
working undercover like spies
meeting in a St Petersburg bunker,
acidophilus as intelligence
to what happens down there—the churning bass
keeping rhythm as deep river.
Sometimes digestion wars like the Congo,
sometimes it's like a Tibetan mantra
creating meditative serenity
despite big city pressure, and the two
alternate as reading of my stress
busy like traffic filtering
as white noise through a streaming underpass.

Almost Dark

Pre-sleep, my door open onto Sam's floor,
Samantha with her introspective fringe,
red as retrievable sunlight,
we'd play Dylan's grainy climacteric
moody substance-dosed elegy,
nothing to lose, nothing to win
inside the song's resistant ecosphere,
as the compression of my state,
the damage is me still fizzy not flat,
like a bottle stood on its head,
October outside, as brutal sculpture,
in a garden turned defiant vermilion,
the two of us exchanging thoughts like bright
Quality Street wrappers, a purple, gold,
a green, a red, surprises littering
our disclosures, while Dylan played in E,
as a late night soundtrack to admissions
that deepened, little things joined big
spontaneously: we got to know
the troubled things, and down below the calm
beneath it all, locked in our separate beds,
talking across the room divide
about the day's events, a dress she saw
in Liberty, but couldn't buy,
and of a moment we shared earlier,
watching through tie-dyed clouds a shocking pink
deepening to a raspberry slab
annotated by a grey evening sky.

Moon Gangs

A sky full of retro-flare signatures,
orbiting fixtures from the moon hotel,
a rival lunar gang nuked the Hilton,
their gadgetry-studded combat helmets
twinkling with industry. Dean watched it all,
the shuttle incinerated on its pad,

space tourist hostages in silver suits
threatened with disconnect, securicams
smashed with plasma rifles, all datastacks
deactivated, the hotel's alarm
wailing towards a dusty mountain range,
the siren like an urgent car-horn jammed

after a head-on with a concrete pillar.
They'd left in a square-faced hospital truck,
porthole windows and caterpillar treads,
tractored their way into a Utah zone
accelerating into greyed-out haze:
most captives dead from cardiac arrest,

the torched atrium detonating flame.
Dean hung on, waiting for the rescue ship,
the burns like blackened omelettes on his hands,
space paramedics treating him on board.
Back home, he screened himself with aviators,
brokered chat-show interviews, grew obsessed

with Onassis memorabilia,
Jackie's cold rocks gifted by a gangster
and worn with glacial frigidity.
Mostly, he feared revenge, the gang's return
from Mhlongo, Osupile or Angkor Wat,
the fortress car so techno-military

he'd known its insides as a weapons lab?
At night, he listened through crate-sized speakers
to frequencies emitted by deep space
like hearing an egg fry in stereo.
His cat would bristle like a black cactus.
He'd shoot it half his tranquillising jab.

He'd heard rumours of the gang's corpse locker,
stuffed full of astronauts and NASA parts,
and the fortress-tracking radar,
and downloaded his genes, and lay awake,
hearing his heartbeat amplified, his brain
fucked by the radio-leak of a rogue star.
SF Drugs

An ice-cream pink Mercedes rips the road,
a 600 SL that disappears
fast as a rocket launch rejection-phase,
chauffeuring a burnt-out rock dinosaur?
The two who track it, she's in purple boots,
and he looks mutant, redesigned android,

head busy with fuzzy automata,
sit by a black Mitsubishi Space star.
His laptop boots-up info from his cult—
the password Super Ballard: mauve lenses,
pink cropped hair, a star tattooed on the cock,
shoulder bags crammed with pharmaceuticals

they're inner-space invaders brokering
a present in which girl gangs terrorise,
injecting infected HIV blood
into their carjacked victims. Mister Rip,
the EuroUK-synthesised autocrat,
(medical history: paranoid schizoid)

presides over underground galleries,
the last HQ was vacuumed into space:
the blow-out blasting through the stratosphere.
They sit and chill: the day breaks up in blocks,
mediated space-times that seem to shift
dimension like film sequences. Her boots

terminate in an indigo mini.
He hacks news of an air traffic shutdown,
jammed satellite transmission frequencies:
the leaders grounded in secure compounds
and bomb-proof warrens. They take SF drugs
that come up as UFO lexicon,

the chemical writing in saucer shapes
in purple, green and orange. It's an hour's
duration, a flip through the galaxy,
followed by a re-entry drug, Blue Sky,
in which adaptation's made like sugar spooned
in crystallised free fall into coffee.

They've lit a fire, and feel the substance cool.
Her lipstick melts on him like red toothpaste.
Their neural networks cohere, and the sun
breaks through the pixellated atmosphere.
They move on to the cult's next convention,
all Europe burning, but inner space won.

Antivenom

Her fingernails are orange lollipops
scrolling for antivenom remedies,
the sunset outside, lurid purple-red,
like the cover of a sci-fi paperback,
aliens swarming from a doughnut-shaped ship
into a solar meltdown? She clicks search
on venomous toxic proteins—
saliva ejected from needling fangs
to hit the nerves like a blackout shutdown,
the bite like instant electrocution.
He's out there, and she pictures it,
fist locked round the head of a rattlesnake,
a wrangler lashed by a rope-thick cobra,
his silver Ford Ranger Thunder
parked up extraterrestrially
in strangulating bush. 20 bites in,
he's used to being banged out flat,
the neurotoxins grabbing at his blood.
She sequences messenger RNA
transcribed from cells, and hitches at the belt's
Peruvian turquoise support
above her skinny washed-out low-rise jeans.
The sunset again, and the SF cover's changed
to strawberry, black and lemon-green
eruptions; and her chromium lamp
comes on as a familiar domestic planet
against dark matter in between the stars.
It's the hormone in Stephen's banded snake
she researches, (it's patented)
for regulating human blood pressure.
His text comes: minimal, upbeat, and she
looks out at a pomegranate fireball
swallowed into deep space, shuts down and runs
towards the future in the flaming sky.

People Who Don't Die

Forgotten Poems

Downgrade in little magazines
secured by staples fragile as earrings,
with names like *Joe DiMaggio*,
Little Caesar, or *Ant's Forefoot*,
the work's suspended cryogenically,
unnoticed as gold metal room numbers
in a red carpeted hotel
corridor in Shinjuku or Mayfair?
Sometimes I break in like a tomb-raider
randomly scaring up contents,
the expendable and the resistant
anthologised as DNA traces
to underground lyric circa whatever?
(vintage small mag 1978?)—
Little Caesar. Lou Reed on the cover.

I search John Wieners for his air
of hitting bottom note that blue
the poem hums like a piano
after the singer's gone:
turn up Joe Brainard and James Schuyler too
in my accessible quota
of quirky underground instructors:
the motive all composed around
a visual image retrieved earlier—
of a neighbour's urn of purple pansies
grouped together like a raised umbrella
positioned on the entrance steps
to 103 South Hill Park Gardens,
the stucco crumbling like lowgrade,
depleted ink, the inconsistencies
showing up like a badly inked slow fade.

Cape Goliard
for Tony Frazer

It's the damped glue and paper smell—
the Barry Hall letterpress bite,
the retro fonts staring me down
 opening out tight chocolate boards
in a brown Joe Brainard pansies wrapper

10x6 not 8x5
book statistics, Tom Raworth's *Moving*—
the words so fast they're substances
metabolised by reading.
Back home I reacquaint myself

with books coffined for 30 years,
pristine mortuary deposits
left untouched, as though mummified
in tissue, their bright dust jackets
a paper pharaoh's funeral clothes,

hieroglyphs coded into ISBNs.
My purchases were sunny days,
the future like a delayed flight,
the present full of quantum mix,
chewed sunglasses' frames, coffee froth,

the luxury of beach days spent
tweaking volcanic sand grains with my toes:
the light indexed on golden hairs,
my body ripening in the sun,
floppy petunias bleeding into scent.

Those books broke open on my youth
dust-jackets like pop wallpaper,
declassifying poetry.
I learnt from them, then went away
leaving them stashed in a cupboard

like retrievable gold bars:
no nick or warp in their time-lagged
redundancy, and viewed again
are crisp as cutting an apple,
skin polished by the summer rain.

Beautiful Losers

A frontal slash on *Beautiful Losers*,
the Barry Hall jacket, ruched, cut,
split like a Yamamoto dress
the scarlet lettering a poppy red
triangulated hot caption—

the author's name Leonard Cohen
upper right, a floaty tomato red,
the book a British first
1970: ISBN
224 61833 4:

its looks harnessed to its decade,
wears random damage, like error
accumulating in my cells
as unrecordable biography.
The cover nude's in soft bondage—

silk ribbons tied round a torso
from which a cratered nipple peaks
like a snail putting out in rain.
I read it by rapid excerpt
like sitting backwards on a train

tracking familiar things wrong way
into a composite topology.
Jacket repairs are optional:
I like the lacerated strips,
like a resistant fly poster

outliving its redundancy.
I knew that text once, slugged it out with Scotch
on ribs of a deserted beach,
the wear and tear begun there, the whisky
red as a chestnut in my glass.

Death Tourism

At 17 I went there and came back
a fist full of diazepam
soggy like sky-blue impasto,
granulated chemical blues
the colour of the shirt I wear today
instructing me into whiteout

not blackout states, like moon-walking
in zero-gravity.
I needed to get back before
my oxygen supply ran out,
resistant pressure in my cells
detaining me

like I'd got trapped behind the exit door
in a free fall plane crash
bottoming out on fried wasteland.
Someone was there, but grainily,
no ID recognition in their face
blurred as a hangover take

of writing on a cereal box.
My time in disconnect stays clear
as a lime canoe
bopping like a life-boat in gin,
no signposts, mapping, brain read-out,
just gravitational pull into a corridor

bumpy with air-pocketing.
I never came out right again,
even adjustments showed the kink
as though I was an in-between,
someone who'd defected from life
but never made it into death,

a re-modified human,
dodgy with the weird signature
of those who'd crossed over.
Sometimes I see it behind drink
the familiar hurt in a friend
shattered from having been there

and nervous that his hidden scar
shows through like an internal bruise
as a questionable survivor
like me, of falling off the world
and making a dazed re-entry,
like wave-patterns running up the spine.

Syd's Dead

A lolling purple iris, split open
into streaming gold nebulae,
he stands back from the canvas, measures it
for approximate memory
then smashes it over a bony knee,
an art house self-destruct, preserve nothing
but the renewed impulse for creativity,
and walks away from the toe-punched debris
into the kitchen, (a Cambridge semi),
and jugs a waspish cider from the fridge.
His epitaph's painted in red on the ceiling—
Syd Barrett 1966–68,
subsequently alive, but posthumous?
Two years as the permed, madcap acid-head,
smudged black eyeliner, violet eyes,
LSD dropped in his coffee and tea,
psychosis escalating like jungle lianas
streaming with flashback imagery—
a snake evolving from a banana,
a gold-skinned shaman sitting in a tree?
He got it down in nursery rhymes, three chords,
a UFO club psychedelic residency:
and exploded like a burnt-out quasar
and blew it all the way he did with art,
fast as randomly throwing a flaming guitar
into a swimming pool. Then, years of it,
provincial ennui, the ultimate
disappearing act, not in the desert,
but donnish Cambridge, Grantchester Meadows
providing rainy ruminative solitude
for blackout moods, perhaps a kingfisher
darting a sapphire at his look,
the years de-realising, hunting round
for little clues, like nothing in particular,
but acorns, shopping lists, a spiny leaf
parachuting its red silks to the ground?

The Last Experience

The objectless smile of rock's polymath,
the Albert Hall, 24/2/69,
the cold outside like white Siberia
implanted into black cab fuzzy Kensington,
Hendrix's stratospheric Fender Stratocaster
tuned like a Formula One Ferrari,
gunning his riffs through the sound barrier
on 'Foxy Lady', 'Purple Haze',
the pyrotechnical LSD repertoire,
'Room Full Of Mirrors', 'Sunshine of Your Love',
his virtuoso chord-changes sounding
like gearbox selectors on a Silverstone bend,
shifting down on a low bluesy 'Hey Joe',
played like he's in a windowless hangar
or confessing last regrets on Death Row:
the sadness touches on dereliction.
Jimi's fuzzed perm's nailed by a bandana,
his purple shirt's ruffled like a surf hem,
his pencil-line moustache defined
like a girl's eyebrow. The Experience
push hard behind him as an undertow,
that can't catch up, manic percussion, heartbeat bass
smashing into the synthesis
like cars impacting head-on, fire-gutted
into sonic detonation.
They knob-twiddle; he coaxes his fretboard
to a sneaky voodoo, a stoned riff contoured
to match the drug inside his brain.
He plays a right-handed guitar, left hand,
revving the noise, blowing volume control,
smashes his guitar on a stack,
turns round, resumes, the fine-tuned substitute
played like live nerves, the thing howling feedback,
as Jimi rips into 'Foxy Lady'
tooled like a supernova roaring fire through space.

Saint Derek of Dungeness

   The light on its arrival travels at the speed of thought
186,000 miles per second, like the image clicked on
in the brain's neural microcircuitry.
                      A Whiteout—Derek Jarman's
                           dead,
              molecularized into a space-time
              I can't see, a blue or red
                      dispersal
              of chemical activity.
              His poppers hit into his blood
                  as a potent mutagen
              in Soho— Derek's
                      halo
              of N-nitroso compounds
              shining bright.

The sea's always arriving like the universe accelerating
hot rocks in space. When Russell digitally reorganizes
light at Dungeness I find I see what I imagine.
                I ask him
do the dead get numbers, like the computer RGB
coordination of white as 225, 255, 255? It's a process
called additive mixing, in this case created by integrating
approximate intensities of the primary colours of light—
red, green and blue.
                      A whiteout—Derek Jarman's
                         blue
              ink's still raised on letters sent
              me in his viral meltdown
                    size zero
              on AZT—a bamboo waist in jeans
              his journals recreating each moment
                  as optimal
              event, like my rhyming Zidovudine
                  (generic AZT)
              with orange sunshine.

White areas are the absence of ink on the paper.
Russell walks in and out of a fog pocket—white tips of tangy
sea mist smoking over crunched shingle shot through with leathery
purple shoots of sea kale (crambe martina). His camera's the
extension of his neurology—it's the intelligence through which
he sees digitally.

      Russell re-appears,
    Derek's not coming through,
    the light that he contacts
     is red green and blue
    co-ordinated into white. The fog disappears
    like a double helix, a grey pretzel
      involved in the pattern
    of this ecosphere.
    Derek's got no passband no
      wavelength frequency,
    the grey horizon finds a soft dissolve
      in a slinky grey sea.

Derek was sainted on Dungeness beach by the Sisters of Perpetual
Indulgence (SPI), radical genderfuck activists, his
canonisation as a gay icon St Derek of Dungeness of the
Order of Celluloid Knights staged as a ritual healing
ceremony in 1994.

      Saint now

          go

  When photons travel at the speed of light time and
space disappear as light is unaffected by gravity. If a photon
weighs the estimate is 4×10^{-48} grams, with an electron
having a mass of 9×10^{-22} grams.

     A man sits with a mug of tea
      crumpled on the shore
     his red exit sign apparent
     from his viral load, the roar
       in his veins

> a toxic cosh for toxo
> sarcomas and nuking free radicals
> > his life come to this
> thin as the horned yellow poppy
> with its A-line silk skirts
> shattered on the beach
> even connecting two thoughts laterally
> hard to reach.
> > Saint Derek of Dungeness
> shivering under a sky turned lipstick red
> knowing he can't shoot or talk back
> > dead.

If you moon-walked you'd find footprints left by visiting
astronauts still not dusted over by meteoric grit, but Derek's
bootmarks have been irretrievably rubbed out on Dungeness
beach, Old Compton Street, Soho, the footpaths behind Jack Straw's
Castle on Hampstead's East Heath, his treads and
DNA signature wiped by successive walk-overs.

> When Russell came into Red Snapper Books today
the Dungeness light was circulating through his body as
> > gold.
> > Cold gold heated by blood
to energy—
> > if you implant gold nanoparticles into
tissue particles to measure the electrical activity of live
neurons, the neuronal activity modulates the electron
density at the surface of the nanoparticle, which causes
a resonance at visible/near-infrared wavelengths.

> Purple taupe and Davy's grey
> shimmer as dusty radiation
> over the slow-swimming bay

White light stimulates all three types of colour sensitive
> cone cells in the human eye

in near equal amount and with high brightness compared
                to the surroundings

        A poem's a habit
        I feed with neural impulses
        and colours violet
        orange green and blue
        like a drug comes up
        mediating altered states
        as its active resources,
        Derek in it today
        as a chemical re-mix
        the image out of focus
        I do what I do
                      baby blue

  Russell's photos bring Derek's absence in. Their shimmering,
powdery, atmospheric luminosity tracks light without
biomass like printing
                white on white
 or rose taupe, lavender or magnolia light
 greys are the aliens in with us today

        Derek wanted to film
        my novel on Lautréamont Isidore
        in a mirrored bathroom
        on a purple slashed floor
        ISBN 9755451102
        the dodgy operative
        from Montevideo
        self-harmed at 21
        an OD or murder
        behind a locked hotel door
        after writing Maldoror
        as seminal punk

        eating rat in the Paris siege
        or dead drunk.
        I never got paid for the book
        it's open for a movie
        shot in the dull glinting light
        of Isidore's last room key

        (Death Certificate No. 2028)
Isidore Ducasse died on Thursday 24 November 1870,
in his hotel room at 7 Faubourg-Montmartre, his death
certificate signed by the hotel proprietor J.F. Dupuis
and A. Milleret one of his staff.

        Saint now
                go

Dungeness Blues

He stands by the track
a prescription in his hand
quartz mica basalt granules
grooved from the sand
under his Doc Martens
bumped up lymph glands
a face gone in
pointing to the bone
alone
the train late
the clouds signposting rain
oh if he had a date
or moment of hope
round as an orange
of life expectancy
to recharge his aura
with rainbow bands
he'd sing it as lyric
into the light
right in himself not sick
in a viral sweat
his defences broken down
by a replicating trick
copied in his cells
Derek go home
if there's such a place
skinny in the waiting
as a tomato stick

White Associations

The White Room   Lee Harwood (Fulcrum 1969)
  rolling hallucinated heat in the backrooms of Paris bookshops
The Rolling Stones *Beggars Banquet*
  the white RSVP sleeve a slogan on sneering muddy blue blues
White camelias
  the doubles splashed pink in my first publisher's garden at
  Haut du Hont
White Fog
  Smoking over Russell like atomised pearl on his white Sandgate
  beach
White Valium 10mg (Indian)
  The best benzo do glittering a mood. Made by Nicholas
  Piramal under license from Roche, like diamond dust on
  the receptor sites. Indians don't dye pharmaceuticals.
White on White
  The sky when I look out from writing poetry in.
  Sauvignon Blanc
  It tastes like white sunlight poured out chilled
Yellow.
White shirts
  A cool band thing with spearpoint collars and oceans
  of cuff.
White jackets
  Creating space on the Keith Cunningham designed dust
  jackets for Anna Kavan novels, white as the heroin
  prescribed her by Dr Bluth
Hollen Street
  The white surround on London street signs—this one
  lettered Hollen Street W1   City of Westminster

Geography

Place displaces body space
I become what I see
Prospect Cottage in grainy light
its hoodoo anomalies
like malleable voodoo

                                                  blue blue blue

in Derek's wiry garden
a rootless mortuary
his illness burning out
his immunity
like cell hoodoo-voodoo

                                   blue blue blue

an endgame directed
without equality
at a resistant end.
I sniff the beach smell like reality
seaweed as a green redo

                                   blue blue blue

a badlands with a lighthouse
like a stripy Polo mint
and optimal exposure
to Siberian crossover
a bite that's so blue

                                   blue blue blue

I'm there to renew contact
like neuroimaging
with Derek's dispersal
if he has a signal
it's green and red and blue

                             blue blue blue

The light keeps arriving
tracking in from space
lavender and violet
colouring consciousness
it always gets through

                           blue blue blue

TOMORROW AS TODAY

Moondust

The light's the colour of moondust
scattering sunlight, moon impact craters
sandblasted by micrometeorites,
a foggy, grainy snakeskin grey
the tangy English Channel in the mist
dissolving into white on white

Dungeness shimmer as the day
fizzes like Aspirin in a glass—
granules dispersed like a contrail
zipping an opalescent churn.
Light's a diffused chemical mix
its integration of blue and red flux

arriving as a photon pulse
over a place themed by the sea's
cool grey that's greenish Xanadu—
(Resene chart colour code 5G050)
trainspotter grey, aerospace grey,
colouring thought with gravity

like the corrugated constructs,
wooden sheds grouped so randomly
they're like a concentration camp
broken up by its detainees,
a flatland with nuclear power stations
reminding that alien intelligence

gets smart implant everywhere
as though martians had chipped the coast
from Dungeness, to Pett Level and Hythe.
I come back to the shingled beach
its platform under a white sky
littered with found art, sculptured twists

of metal, bone and banged in bits
as unconverted trash
like NASA junk left on the moon,
PLSS backpacks, rovers, footprints—
the stuff that's never coming back
and sighted by bright sunlight glints

like heavy lunar industry
in microgravity, cement
compacted there, while reactors
dominate a powdery Kent coastline
that's filmed by universal light
and coming up right starts to shine.

Baudelaire and the 21ˢᵗ Century

1
He's solid, like Harrods or Selfridges,
his book a mutable pathology
replicated in the poetic gene:

a case history projected in quatrains.
Les Fleurs du mal worked on as autopsy
to a confected, nugget translation.

2
The book's a 102 carat black diamond
shot with sparkle like a swimming pool,
the universe exploding at its core.

It's corroded like a disused urinal
submerged beneath the street, a site recalled
for intimate contact with marble stalls.

3
A black frilly tulip sheened like plum-skin,
that's Jeanne Du Val with lolling orange tongue,
resistant to Baudelaire's STD:

a gonococcal infection
treated with neuro-toxic mercury:
the outlawed poet in viral meltdown.

4
Baudelaire's name's like a diagnosis
for a depressed state in brain chemistry.
He's mood-themed to rainy autumnal days

walking deserted quays, the rain's simmer
releasing tiny silver parachutes
on impact with the river's taut grey silk.

5
The anti-careerist with dyed green hair,
we rehabilitate his attitude
of defiantly endgaming urban

experience into something terminal
that won't go down, the visionary present,
bullet-proof as a pilot's cockpit door.

6
His lapidary words, they're like building blocks
we reassemble. Fill a black condom
with unquarantined moon-dust

and that's a Baudelaire sonnet:
the sparkle in the pathogens,
a colour always elicited from regret.

7
Baudelaire's gnomic opium data:
minimal 150 drops a day
in addict speak, rock bottom apathy.

He lives on as post-biological,
an image-bank we dip into
like shooting film of a dead man dreaming.

8
The poet without income: how to write
with a cryogenic account:
all credit frozen? It's his fiscal legacy,

to pour a Nuit St Georges like a black sun,
eat nothing, but appoint his lines
a 28" waist, Rolling Stones durable legacy.

9
Black suit, black tie, the man rehabilitated black.
His epitaph's a florist's dark red rose
left on the pavement. Who will pick it up?

His gene-code spills into the night river.
The poetry's forensic: liver, spleen.
A barge churns by like unzipping a dress.

www.ingramcontent.com/pod-product-compliance
Lightning Source LLC
Chambersburg PA
CBHW031157160426
43193CB00008B/404